D1435621

MAY YOU ENJOY THIS BOOK

The Public Library is free to all cardholders. You can increase its usefulness to all by returning books promptly, on or before the "Date Due"

If you derive pleasure and profit from the use of your public library, please tell others about its many services.

THE NASHUA PUBLIC LIBRARY
2 COURT STREET
NASHUA, NH 03060

PARROTS

Please visit our web site at: www.garethstevens.com
For a free color catalog describing Gareth Stevens Publishing's
list of high-quality books and multimedia programs, call
1-800-542-2595 (USA) or 1-800-387-3178 (Canada).
Gareth Stevens Publishing's fax: (414) 332-3567.

Library of Congress Cataloging-in-Publication Data available upon request from publisher.
Fax (414) 336-0157 for the attention of the Publishing Records Department.

ISBN 0-8368-4122-0

This edition first published in 2004 by
Gareth Stevens Publishing
A World Almanac Education Group Company
330 West Olive Street, Suite 100
Milwaukee, Wisconsin 53212 USA

Editorial and design: Tucker Slingsby Ltd., London
Gareth Stevens series editor: Catherine Gardner
Gareth Stevens art direction: Tammy Gruenewald

Picture Credits
NHPA — Stephen Dalton: 7, 8, 19, 25; Gerard Lacz: 11; Haroldo Palo, Jr.: 12;
    Kevin Schafer: 13, 17; Mirko Stelzner: 15 (both), 16, 18, 24, 25; Bill Coster:
    18; James Carmichael, Jr.: 23; Martin Harvey: 23; Martin Wendler: 23, 28;
    Dave Watts: 27.
Oxford Scientific Films — Manfred Pfefferle: cover, title page, 6; Niall Benvie: 9, 19;
    Konrad Wothe: 9, 19; Michael Fogden: 12; Tui De Roy: 14, 22; Michael Sewell:
    20-21; Paul Franklin: 21; Bob Gibbons: 21; Wendy Shattil and Bob Rozinski: 26;
    Robin Bush: 27; Michael Powles: 27; Max Gibbs: 28-29; Howie Garber: 29.

Printed in the United States of America

1 2 3 4 5 6 7 8 9 08 07 06 05 04

PARROTS

Gareth Stevens Publishing
A WORLD ALMANAC EDUCATION GROUP COMPANY

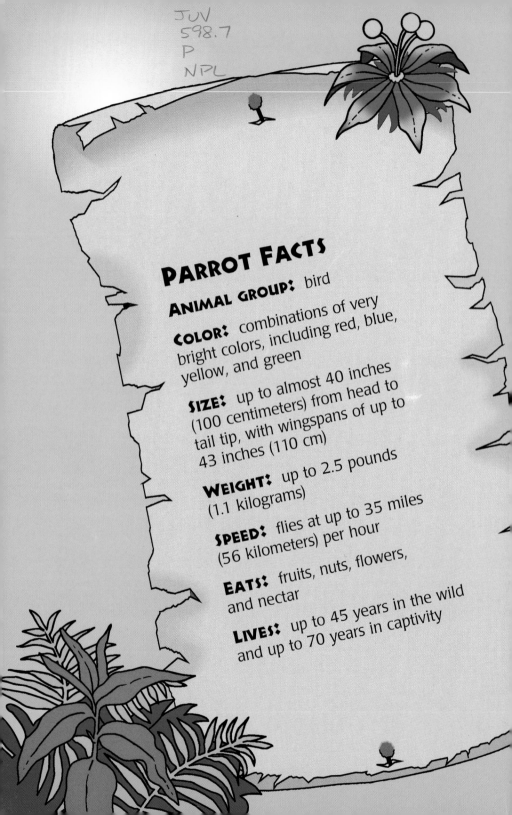

Parrot Facts

Animal Group: bird

Color: combinations of very bright colors, including red, blue, yellow, and green

Size: up to almost 40 inches (100 centimeters) from head to tail tip, with wingspans of up to 43 inches (110 cm)

Weight: up to 2.5 pounds (1.1 kilograms)

Speed: flies at up to 35 miles (56 kilometers) per hour

Eats: fruits, nuts, flowers, and nectar

Lives: up to 45 years in the wild and up to 70 years in captivity

CONTENTS

Words that appear in the glossary
are printed in **boldface** type the
first time they occur in the text.

A Closer Look

Parrots are colorful birds with curved **bills**. From the top of the head to the tip of the tail, they can be as long as 40 inches (100 centimeters) or as short as 4 inches (10 cm). Macaws, parakeets, lovebirds, and cockatoos are some well-known kinds of parrots.

Like all birds, parrots have two legs, two wings, and lots of feathers. Birds are the only animals with feathers. The feathers protect their bodies and keep them warm.

DID YOU KNOW?

• Birds do not have teeth. They have bills, or beaks, instead.

• A bird's bill is made from the same material as a human's fingernail.

• A bird's bill never stops growing.

• Most parrots can move their lower jaws from side to side as well as up and down.

I have a flexible neck, so I can turn my head around to clean my back with my bill.

My large, strong wings help me fly through the air.

My body is covered with lots of brightly colored feathers.

My bill is strong enough to crack open hard nuts.

My tail is almost as long as my body.

The ends of my toes are sharp claws called talons. They help me hold onto branches and food.

A parrot's rounded head is covered with feathers. Its eyes are on the sides of its head, so it can see almost everything around it and can spot danger, in any direction, very quickly. Its ears are hard to see because they are covered with feathers and do not stick out the way human ears do. While a parrot's hearing is excellent, its sense of smell is poor. Its **nostrils** are at the top of its bill.

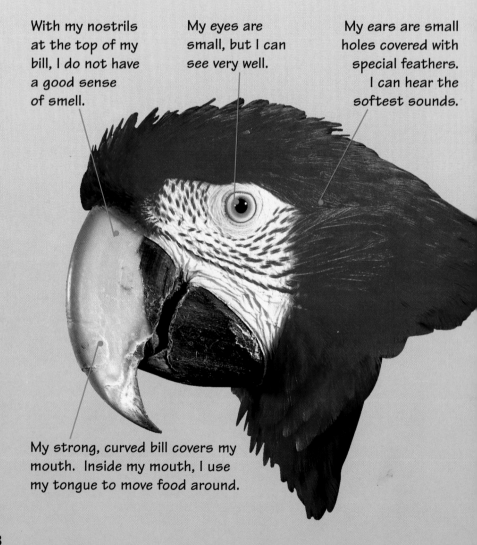

With my nostrils at the top of my bill, I do not have a good sense of smell.

My eyes are small, but I can see very well.

My ears are small holes covered with special feathers. I can hear the softest sounds.

My strong, curved bill covers my mouth. Inside my mouth, I use my tongue to move food around.

HANDY BILLS

A parrot's bill is extremely useful. The bird uses it to crush seeds, to **preen,** and to clean its mate and its babies. A big bill is great for removing nasty **parasites** and for smoothing body oils along feathers. The bill also works like a third foot to help the parrot climb.

TOUGH TOES

A parrot has four strong toes on each foot. Two point forward, and two point backward, so the parrot can easily pick up objects and hold them. Its special toes also help the parrot grip tree branches tightly. A parrot can hang from a branch by one foot and reach out to pick a juicy piece of fruit with the other!

Home, Sweet Home

The macaw is a large, colorful parrot that lives in the tropical rain forests of Central America and South America. In these forests, the air and soil are always warm and wet, so most of the plants there grow all year long. Rain forests have more kinds of plants and animals than any other place in the world. The rain forests, however, are being cut down to build homes and farms and to get lumber for furniture and firewood for cooking and for heating houses. As the forests disappear, the macaws and other animals that need rain forests for food and shelter are in danger.

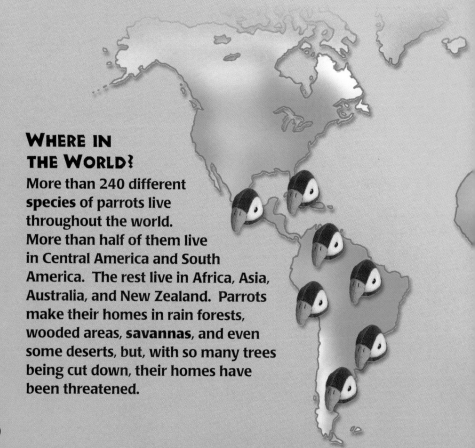

Where in the World?

More than 240 different **species** of parrots live throughout the world. More than half of them live in Central America and South America. The rest live in Africa, Asia, Australia, and New Zealand. Parrots make their homes in rain forests, wooded areas, **savannas**, and even some deserts, but, with so many trees being cut down, their homes have been threatened.

Many people think that the first birds developed from small, meat-eating dinosaurs. **Fossils** show that the earliest kind of bird, called *archaeopteryx*, lived about 150 million years ago. It had feathers and could fly, but its teeth, its skull, and some of its bones were more like the teeth, skull, and bones of a dinosaur.

FLYING JEWELS

Most parrots stay high in the leafy **canopy** of the rain forest. The bright colors of their feathers help them see each other even far away.

NEIGHBORS

Parrots share the forests with many amazing animals. Noisy monkeys and scaly lizards climb through the trees. Spiders, huge beetles, and brightly colored frogs hide under leaves. Tiny hummingbirds and brilliant butterflies flit among the flowers. Hungry **predators**, such as eagles, snakes, and jaguars, keep a sharp lookout for **prey**.

COOL COLORS

The colors of a butterfly protect it from predators, so, depending on what colors they are, different butterflies fly at different levels of the rain forest. Bright blue butterflies are usually high in the treetops, where their shades of blue blend in with the shadows. Striped butterflies are hard to see in the patchy light among the leaves below the canopy. Near the ground, butterflies with see-through wings most easily escape the watchful eyes of predators.

SLOW SLOTH

The sloth is an animal that spends nearly all its life hanging upside down! It grips the branches with its large, hooklike claws as it munches on leaves and fruit. A sloth moves very slowly, crawling along branches at a top speed of only $1/2$ mile (1 kilometer) per hour.

TERRIFIC TAILS

Spider monkeys hang around the top level of a rain forest — often by their tails! They can swing by their tails or legs when they feed, keeping their hands free to pick juicy fruit from the tips of branches.

CANOPY

Hummingbirds fly through the leafy treetops, collecting nectar from flowers.

LIFE AT ALL LEVELS

Animals live everywhere in a rain forest, from the ground to the treetops.

UNDERSTORY

Ocelots hunt smaller animals in the rain forest. These spotted wildcats often sleep on the branches of trees.

UNDERGROWTH

Armadillos dig up the forest floor to find insects and other kinds of food.

13

THE FAMILY

Even though they usually live as pairs or in small family groups, parrots are very **social** birds. As they fly, they call to each other with loud, ear-splitting screams. At the times of the day when they feed or **roost**, hundreds of parrots may gather together. In the early morning, large **flocks** of parrots fly through the forest in search of food. In the evening, just before the sun sets, they return to the places where they roost.

Parrots are good parents. They build safe, cozy nests for their young, usually in tree holes that are sometimes more than 100 feet (30 meters) above the ground. Most female parrots lay eggs every two or three years, but some kinds wait four years between raising groups of young. After laying eggs, the female keeps them warm until they hatch, which takes about four weeks. Females lay their eggs so they will hatch at the time of year when food is easiest to find. Both males and females gather fruit and nuts to feed their babies, which are called chicks.

UGLY DUCKLING

Newly hatched parrots are not as pretty as their parents! They look like little bundles of skin, at first, but do not stay that way for long. Their feathers soon begin to grow, and by the time the chicks are six months old, they are almost as big and as bright as their parents.

Baby File

Birth

Parrots have one to four babies at a time. When the chicks first hatch, they have few feathers and cannot see. After about two weeks, their feathers start to grow and the chicks open their eyes. Parrot parents pick food, hold it in their bodies, and let it start to **digest**. Then, they go back to the nest and feed the chicks the partly digested food.

Two to Six Months

Little parrots grow up fast. By the time they are ten weeks old, the chicks have grown lots of feathers, and their wings and tails have almost reached their full size. At about four months old, the chicks are ready to leave the nest and make their first flights. When parrot chicks are six months old, they are almost the same size as their parents.

One to Two Years

Even when they are full size, young parrots still have a lot to learn. They usually stay with their parents for up to two years while they learn how to fly, what to eat, and how to avoid enemies. They also learn how to find the best places to feed and to roost. Their parents will not raise another **clutch** until the young parrots have left home.

LIFE ON THE WING

Flocks of parrots glide almost silently through the rain forest on their huge wings. Like most birds, their light bodies and smooth, streamlined shape help them fly. Birds are lightweight for their size because their bones are hollow and full of air. If a bird is too heavy, it cannot fly. Parrots move around by walking and climbing as well as by flying.

FLYING RAINBOWS

Besides being so colorful, a parrot's wings, like the wings of all other birds, are a special shape. They are rounded on top and curved underneath. This shape is called an airfoil. The airfoil shape helps lift the bird into the air as it flaps its wings and keeps the bird soaring and gliding until it is ready to land.

Birds have several different kinds of feathers. Closest to their bodies, they have a layer of down feathers. The down feathers are very fine and soft. They help keep the bird warm. Down feathers are covered with oily body feathers. The oily feathers keep out the wet and the cold. Birds also have long wing feathers that help lift them into the air to fly. At times, birds **molt**, or lose their feathers. After molting, they grow new feathers.

LANDING GEAR

Parrots use their long tail feathers to help them steer when they are in the air and balance when they are on the ground. When a parrot is ready to land, its tail feathers fan out and act like a brake to slow down the bird's flight.

FAVORITE FOODS

Parrots feast on fruits, nuts, flowers, and nectar. They often eat unripe fruits and nuts that other animals leave alone. The macaw is a great nutcracker! Its special, hooked bill can break open even a hard Brazil nut. First, it uses the edge of its bill like a saw to cut partway through the nutshell. Then, with one bite of its super-strong bill, it cracks the shell open.

CLAY TIME!

Along with the fruits and nuts they usually eat, some kinds of parrots eat clay, which is a type of soil. Hundreds of parrots gather at clay pits along riverbanks and take turns clawing up clay to eat. No one knows for sure why parrots eat clay. Some people think the clay helps break down poisons found in the unripe fruit the birds eat.

TRICKY TONGUES

A parrot often holds its food in its claws while it eats. Once the parrot has lifted the food up to its bill, it can no longer see the food. It uses its thick, flexible tongue to judge the shape of the food and to move the food around in its mouth. When the food is in the perfect position, the parrot crushes the food with its strong, hard bill.

TALL TREES

Thousands of different kinds of plants grow in tropical rain forests, and parrots are willing to taste almost any of them. Although most kinds of parrots do not seem to be picky about what they eat, they do have favorite foods, which include the nuts and seeds of giant mahogany, kapok, coral bean, and rubber trees.

DID YOU KNOW

- The top and bottom of a parrot's bill rub against each other, which helps keep the edges sharp.

- Even when young parrots can feed themselves, they still behave like babies and beg their parents to get food for them.

DANGER!

Some kinds of parrots have more enemies than others. A parrot as big as an adult macaw has very few predators. Eggs and chicks are always the most in danger.

Humans are a threat to all types of parrots. Native hunters in the rain forests kill parrots for their meat and feathers. Other people capture parrots and sell them as pets. As the rain forests are destroyed, parrots also face the dangers of losing their homes and food supplies.

AIR ATTACK!

The harpy eagle is the largest eagle in the world. Flying high over the forest, it looks for prey — and it hunts parrots! A parrot makes a nice meal for an eagle chick. Harpy eagles will attack even big macaws if they see one flying alone. The eagle grabs its prey with the sharp claws, or talons, on its feet.

OPEN WIDE

An emerald tree boa hangs from a branch, blending in with the leaves. If a young parrot flies close enough, the boa will snatch the bird up in its jaws. When the snake cannot catch a bird, it may slither to a parrot's nest and steal its eggs.

EGG THIEVES

The eggs of parrots and other birds attract many hungry predators. The tayra, an animal that is a lot like a weasel, usually hunts tree squirrels, but it will steal parrot eggs if it gets the chance. The toucan has a huge, long, lightweight bill that can easily reach into a parrot's tree hole to steal the bird's eggs.

A Parrot's Day

5:00 AM

The sky was beginning to get light. I preened my feathers carefully to make sure they were in top flying condition. It would soon be time to look for food.

6:00 AM

As the sun rose, all the other parrots started to shriek. My mate and I joined in the song. I went off to find food while she stayed with our chicks.

7:00 AM

I joined many other parrots flying silently through the forest, looking for food. I spied a coral bean tree full of fruit. My favorite!

9:00 AM

I ate as much as I could, then filled my throat pouch with food and flew back to our tree hole. The chicks were very hungry by the time I arrived. They were squawking loudly and had their bills opened wide for me to feed them. I had enough food for my mate, too.

11:00 AM

I flew to the clay lick near the river. Hundreds of parrots were clawing up sticky clay and flying off to eat it. I screamed loudly to let them know it was my turn!

12:00 NOON

At the clay lick,
I spotted an eagle
flying above us. A group
of us flew toward the eagle,
screaming loudly to chase it away!

2:00 PM

My mate left me with the chicks
while she flew off to look for food.
She brought back another hearty meal.
Chicks are always hungry!

3:00 PM

My mate and I preened each other,
then I flew off to find more food.

5:00 PM

It was nearly sunset. I joined the other parrots and
flew back to our roosting site. We called to each
other loudly as we flew through the forest.

6:00 PM

I fed my mate, then we both fed the
chicks. When the chicks were done
eating, we cleaned them. They
can be very messy eaters!
Raising chicks is hard work.

7:00 PM

Our neighbors have
stopped calling and
chattering. The
forest is silent.
It's time to settle
down and sleep.

Relatives

Hundreds of different kinds of parrots live on Earth. Most have brightly colored feathers and a strong, hooked bill, and they all perch in trees, using their toes to grip the branches. Different kinds of parrots look different, however, and are different sizes. The colors of their feathers range from bright yellow to deep blue, and the 40-inch- (1-m-) long hyacinth macaw is ten times the size of a pygmy parrot. Parrots usually live close to other parrots and use noisy calls to keep in touch.

Let's Talk

Yellow-headed parrots from the Amazon rain forest make loud squawks. They can also **mimic** other sounds and can be taught to talk, so they are popular as pets. So many of these parrots have been taken from the wild that they are now very rare.

Bright Budgies

The budgerigar is one of the smallest Australian parrots. It is also one of the world's best-known parrots. Many people keep "budgies" in cages as pets, but in the wild, budgies do not stay in one location very long. Large flocks are seen flying from place to place over the Australian **bush**.

The kakapo, which is a parrot from New Zealand, cannot fly, but it runs fast, and it climbs well. It also jumps from trees, using its wings like a parachute. Kakapos search for food at night, then sleep all day in cracks between big rocks or in burrows formed by tree roots.

Blue Beauty

The hyacinth macaw is the largest kind of parrot in the world. This big blue bird's huge bill is so sharp it can cut through hard nutshells. The hyacinth macaw lives in Central America and South America, but, today, it is very rare. Only about three thousand of these macaws are left in the wild.

HUMANS AND PARROTS

People have prized parrots for thousands of years. Some ancient peoples, including the Maya and Aztecs, believed that parrots were animal gods, and parrots have been kept as pets since the early 1500s, when explorers brought them to Europe. Today, parrots are in danger because of people. Many kinds of parrots are still being caught and sold as pets, and humans are cutting down forest **habitats** to make room for houses and farms and to harvest lumber.

PRETTY POLLY

Because many parrot species can be taught to "talk," they are very popular as pets — but that is bad news for parrots. To make money, people capture parrots from the wild to sell them as pets. Taking too many parrots from an area, however, threatens all of the parrots in that area. In the past one hundred years, two different kinds of macaws have died out completely. Other kinds of parrots have become rare in the wild and may also die out if people do not try to save them.

TOURIST APPEAL

The good news for parrots is that many people are beginning to understand how important rain forests are, and they are working to save the rain forests and set them aside as national parks. Inside these parks, wild animals and plants are safe from being hunted, captured, or destroyed. National parks also provide work for local people and, by attracting tourists, raise money to help both people and wildlife.

DID YOU KNOW

Scarlet macaws were like gods to the Maya people who lived in Central America hundreds of years ago. To the Maya, scarlet macaws represented daylight and the rising Sun. Many Maya rulers and other important people took the name "Macaw," hoping the name would give them the same power they believed the brilliant bird had.

Glossary

BILLS
The beaks of birds, including the jaws and the hard covering that surrounds the jaws.

BUSH
A large area of dry land, usually with only shrubs and small trees growing on it.

CANOPY
The top layer of the rain forest, mainly the leafy treetops.

CLUTCH
A nest of eggs or a group of chicks that have hatched from eggs.

DIGEST
To break down food so that it can be absorbed into the blood and used by the body.

FLOCKS
Groups of animals, such as birds, that live together.

FOSSILS
The remains of animals or plants from times long past, which have been preserved or embedded in rocks and minerals.

HABITATS
The natural settings in which plants and animals live.

MIMIC
To copy or imitate sounds or actions.

MOLT
To shed an outer covering of skin, hair, or feathers.

NOSTRILS
The openings in a nose or a beak,
through which air is drawn for breathing.

PARASITES
Animals or plants that survive by living and feeding
on or inside of another animal or plant.

PREDATORS
Animals that hunt other animals for food.

PREEN
To clean and smooth the feathers with the beak.

PREY
Animals that another animal hunts and kills for food.

ROOST
To settle down to rest or sleep on a branch or a perch or in a nest.

SAVANNAS
Large, flat grasslands found in warm or tropical parts of the world.

SOCIAL
Friendly and wanting to spend time with others.

SPECIES
Groups of animals in which members
of a group have many of the same
physical features and behaviors
and can mate with each other
to produce offspring.

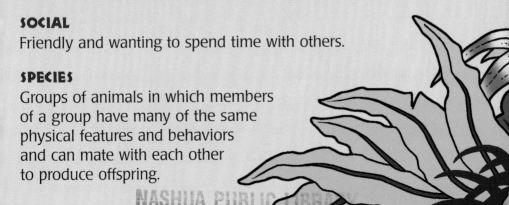

INDEX